Your life as an EXPLORER on a VIKING SHIP

by Thomas Kingsley Troupe

illustrated by Jeff Ebbeler

PICTURE WINDOW BOOKS
a capstone imprint

Thanks to our advisers for their expertise, research, and advice:

Glenn Kranking, PhD, Assistant Professor of History & Scandinavian Studies
Gustavus Adolphus College, Saint Peter, Minnesota

Terry Flaherty, PhD, Professor of English
Minnesota State University, Mankato

Editor: Jill Kalz
Designer: Ashlee Suker
Art Director: Nathan Gassman
Production Specialist: Danielle Ceminsky
The illustrations in this book were created with ink and acrylic paint.

Picture Window Books
1710 Roe Crest Drive
North Mankato, MN 56003
877-845-8392
www.capstonepub.com

All books published by Picture Window Books
are manufactured with paper containing at least
10 percent post-consumer waste.

Library of Congress Cataloging-in-Publication Data
Troupe, Thomas Kingsley.
 Your life as an explorer on a Viking ship / by Thomas Kingsley Troupe;
illustrated by Jeff Ebbeler.
    p. cm. — (The way it was)
 Includes index.
 Audience: Grades K-3.
 ISBN 978-1-4048-7160-1 (library binding)
 ISBN 978-1-4048-7252-3 (paperback)
 1. Vikings—Juvenile literature. I. Ebbeler, Jeffrey. II. Title.
 DL66.T76 2012
 948'.022—dc23
                          2011029572

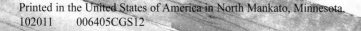

Printed in the United States of America in North Mankato, Minnesota.
102011   006405CGS12

YOUR ROLE

Congratulations! You'll be playing the role of Leif Grimsson, son of Grimr the Grouch, in our play "Life on a Viking Ship." The year is 812. Leif's an 11-year-old boy who is leaving the family farm in Denmark to explore with the Vikings.

Life can be rough at sea. You'll need a strong stomach. But you'll get to see new lands, hear fantastic stories, and maybe snag a few riches.

Ready to sail? **ACTION!**

LEAVING HOME

Horrible Harald is looking for new sailors for his next voyage. With your family's blessing, you eagerly volunteer. Harald asks why you want to leave home when you're so young. "My father is Grimr the Grouch," you tell him. "Before he became a farmer, he sailed the seas. He saw amazing things. I want to see them too!"

"If it's adventure you want, boy," Harald says, "then adventure you'll get!"

Leif, the Vikings loved to go exploring. They sailed all over the place—to France and the British Isles, to Iceland, Greenland, and present-day Newfoundland. They even sailed rivers in eastern Europe all the way to Turkey.

Most Vikings were farmers, but the land could be difficult for growing crops. The search was always on for new, better places to explore and farm.

5

The Vikings carved dragon heads on the prows of their ships to scare enemies. When other sailors saw these fearsome faces, they knew trouble was coming.

BUILDING THE BOATS

On your way to the water, you pass a group of tough shipbuilders. "That's a *knarr*," Horrible Harald says, pointing to the framework. "We use those for trading and long-distance exploring."

"You! Boy!" a man shouts. "Give me a hand." You run over and hold a rough piece of oak while he chips at it with an ax. Other men are fitting the smoothed wood together with nails. They spread a very sticky, thick paste in between the gaps in the wood.

7

THE RAIDING SHIP

At the water's edge sits a longer, thinner ship. **"Here she is,"** Horrible Harald says, **"your new home."** You want to leap aboard and cheer, but the other Vikings look grumpy, so you don't. **"She's called a *drekar*,"** Harald continues. **"She's smaller and faster—perfect for raiding seaside villages."**

The *drekar* ("dragon ship") didn't have rowing benches. Most men simply sat on the chests they brought with them.

MAST
the vertical piece that supports the sail

STERN
the back of the ship

OARS
long paddles used to move the ship when there is no wind; the steering oar is at the back of the ship, right side

The boating term "starboard" likely came from the Vikings. The "steering board" on a Viking longship was on the right side of the ship. Over time, the right side of any boat became known as "starboard."

SAIL
a large sheet usually made of wool

PROW
the front of the ship

HULL
the body of the ship

OAR PORTS
small holes that the oars fit through

CLOTHES MAKE THE MAN

Horrible Harald looks you over and shakes his head. "You're a bit underdressed for this adventure, aren't you, boy?" he says. "You wouldn't last one night on the sea in those clothes." He throws you a thick woolen coat and swatches of fur from a nearby chest. "What are these?" you ask. Harald points to the autumn sky. "When the sun falls, they'll be your best friends."

I know what you're thinking: Where are the **helmets** with the **horns**? Truth is, real Viking helmets didn't have horns. In the 1800s a costume designer created horned helmets for **German operas** about Vikings. The look stuck. La, la, laaa!

Many Viking men wore a *kirtle*, a long shirt that hung to their knees. Vikings often didn't wear shoes. When they did, the shoes were made from animal hide.

ROW, ROW, ROW YOUR BOAT

The ship is loaded, and it's time to head out to sea. You find a spot and grab the handle of an oar. The long oar is tough to move. You're used to hard work, having grown up on a farm. But this is different.

"Row *with* us, boy," Olaf, a big bald Viking, grunts. "Like this." You watch Olaf and time your pull with his. The longship glides through the water. You watch your home grow smaller in the distance.

With a good wind, it took almost three days to get from Denmark to England.

CHOW TIME

You've been rowing for hours. Your arms and back ache. When Horrible Harald shouts, **"Raise the sail!"** the other Vikings cheer. A strong wind blows from the North, moving the ship through the water. No more rowing for a while. Whew!

Someone passes you a hunk of dry, salty fish. **"This is lunch?"** you ask. Olaf slaps your back hard. **"Eat up, boy!"** he shouts. **"You have to keep up your strength!"** You bite into the fish and try not to gag.

Mmm ... Back home you would've had hot, juicy spareribs, legs of lamb, mushrooms, flatbread, and all sorts of flavorful stuff to eat. But it's tough keeping food fresh on a ship. Better get used to **"cold, dry, and salty."**

Very little cooking was done on a longship, for fear of fire. If the Vikings wanted a hot meal, they would head for shore and cook.

A FRIENDLY LITTLE GAME

To pass the time, some of the men play *Hnefatafl*. You watch as Erik's king is trapped in no time. He accuses Svein of cheating and storms off. **"Next!"** Svein shouts, and the men shove you to the game board.

You set up your army of pieces and wait for Svein to move. **"I'm unbeaten, boy,"** Svein warns you. **"Look sharp."** But in three turns, you've cornered his king. Svein pounds the board with his fist, sending pieces flying. **"Next!"** you shout with a hint of a smile.

Hnefatafl was a popular game with the Vikings, though the rules have been lost over time. Some historians believe it was played much like chess. The goal was to trap the other player's king.

WHERE ARE WE?

"We've lost sight of the coastline," Horrible Harald says. You look and see nothing but water in every direction. The wind has died, and the ship rocks gently with the waves. No one is sure where to go.

Olaf checks the water for a current but finds nothing. Erik squints up at the sun and then shrugs. A gull flies across the sky, heading toward the horizon. **"Follow that bird!"** Harald orders. You and the men scramble for the oars.

Some Viking sailors would release ravens (large, black birds) into the sky. The birds would naturally fly to land, and the sailors would follow.

19

STORMS AND STORIES

Black clouds move in. There are flashes of lightning, followed quickly by thunder. "**The mighty Thor grows restless tonight,**" Olaf says. "**It's as if he means to topple mountains with his magic hammer!**"

As the rain begins to fall, Horrible Harald tells a story. You listen to how Thor battled a sea serpent and a giant to win a treasured kettle. The other Vikings add tales of Thor's father, the mighty Odin. The stories take your mind off the storm a bit.

It wasn't until about the 1300s that Viking stories were first written down. Called the Icelandic Sagas, these writings still exist today.

ICELANDIC SAGA

Pay close attention, Leif! You'll be expected to know these stories by heart. The Vikings didn't write down their stories. They passed them orally from generation to generation.

BEDTIME

"**Men,**" Horrible Harald says, "**time to sleep.**"
You lie down on the wooden deck beneath furs and
animal skins. Large waves rock and toss the ship. The
sea air is brutally cold. Shivering, you turn to Olaf.
"**How are we supposed to sleep like this?**"
you ask. But Olaf is already snoring.

CRASH! The ship hits a rough wave. Water splashes
over you, soaking you to the bone.

Some Vikings made
double-wide sleeping
bags out of leather and
slept next to each other
to keep warm.

ARMED FOR BATTLE

After days at sea, Horrible Harald points to the shore. In the distance lies a small village. "We've arrived at last," he says. "Prepare your weapons!"

The Vikings grab swords, axes, and bows and arrows from their sea chests. Olaf pulls a helmet onto his head. He hands you a heavy shield. "Stay behind this, boy," he warns. You're excited but a little scared too. You're going to raid your first village!

Since many Vikings didn't have armor, shields were key to keeping them safe in battle. Most Viking shields were round and made of pinewood.

Earlier in the Viking Age, men brought anything that could be used as a weapon, including farming tools. Later, double-edged swords became the weapon of choice.

ATTACK!

Horrible Harald insists you stay on the ship. **"You're too young for battle, boy,"** he says. **"Maybe next time."** As the longship slides onto the shore, Svein roars a mighty war cry. The Vikings are raiding the village!

You hide behind the shield but peek out a few times. The Vikings shove people out of the way. Erik strikes a man who chooses to fight back. The villagers quickly realize they can't win. They give up and watch as their valuables are stolen from their homes.

Vikings weren't always on the hunt for riches. In some attacks, they took people to sell as slaves. Sometimes they stole the land to farm themselves.

I can't look, Leif. Let me know when it's over. It's well known that Vikings didn't always fight fair. Some would attack at night, while the villagers slept. They would set fire to the houses, then attack the people as they ran out.

SAYING GOOD-BYE

Not all of your shipmates survive the attack. Svein is struck and killed by an arrow. **"He will arrive at Valhalla, the Hall of the Slain,"** Olaf whispers to you. **"That's where our fallen go."**

Horrible Harald and the others place Svein's body, along with his personal items, on a mound of branches and leaves. You add his *Hnefatafl* game. Soon the mound is set on fire. Flames warm your face, and you wonder if you were meant for life on a Viking ship.

The Vikings didn't always burn their dead. Sometimes they buried the fallen man in the ground with all of his things. These items may have included horses, wagons, and anything else that would help him travel to the next world.

CURTAIN CALL

Brilliant! You brought the crowd to its feet! I don't know how you did it, but you perfectly captured Leif's journey. If I didn't know any better, I'd think you really were on a Viking ship.

Now get out there and take a bow!

GLOSSARY

accuse—to blame someone else

current—the movement of water in a river or ocean

drekar—(dray-car) a sleek, fast-moving Viking longship

Hnefatafl—(nef-ah-tah-ful) a Viking board game played much like chess

knarr—(knar) a heavy-cargo Viking longship

orally—by mouth

prow—the front part of a ship; also called a bow

raid—to attack suddenly, without warning

saga—a long, detailed story

INDEX

MORE BOOKS TO READ

Guillain, Charlotte. *Vikings*. Fierce Fighters. Chicago: Raintree, 2010.

Lassieur, Allison. *Life as a Viking: An Interactive History Adventure*. Warriors. Mankato, Minn.: Capstone Press, 2011.

Margeson, Susan M. *Viking*. DK Eyewitness Books. New York: Dorling Kindersley, 2010.

INTERNET SITES

FactHound offers a safe, fun way to find Internet sites related to this book. All of the sites on FactHound have been researched by our staff.

Here's all you do:

Visit *www.facthound.com*

Type in this code: 9781404871601

 Super-cool stuff! Check out projects, games and lots more at **www.capstonekids.com**

LOOK FOR ALL THE BOOKS IN THE SERIES: